THEN & NOW

CHULA VISTA

OPPOSITE: This was Chula Vista's Third Avenue in 1911, looking north. The large building to the left is Farrell's General Store and the U.S. Post Office. The two small buildings in front of the store were the railroad station and the ticket office to serve the trains on Third Avenue. The large building at right is the well-known Melville building. (Courtesy Chula Vista Public Library, Local History Collection.)

THEN & NOW

CHULA VISTA

Frank M. Roseman
and Peter J. Watry

This book has photographs and information that were donated and collected by those who believed in the preservation of the history of our city. We thank them for their thoughtfulness.

Library of Congress Control Number: 2009934866

Published by Arcadia Publishing
Charleston SC, Chicago IL, Portsmouth NH, San Francisco CA

Printed in the United States of America

For all general information contact Arcadia Publishing at:
Telephone 843-853-2070
Fax 843-853-0044
E-mail sales@arcadiapublishing.com
For customer service and orders:
Toll-Free 1-888-313-2665

Visit us on the Internet at www.arcadiapublishing.com

ON THE FRONT COVER: The Memorial Bowl, built during the Great Depression, had a large water feature and seating for several hundred people in an attractive outdoor setting. Almost 75 years later, the water feature has been removed, and a new stage enhances the facility. Memorial Park is dedicated to the fallen service personnel whose names are represented on memorial plaques. (Courtesy Chula Vista Public Library, Local History Collection.)

ON THE BACK COVER: After many decades of being an agricultural community and lemon capital, in 1941, the city changed. The Rohr Aircraft Company moved to Chula Vista, and with demand for workers and housing for them, Chula Vista was on the way to becoming a bedroom community. Frank Roseman and Peter Watry have traced this growth through rare and vintage photographs. (Courtesy Chula Vista Public Library, Local History Collection.)

CONTENTS

ACKNOWLEDGMENTS

This book, like Images of America: *Chula Vista* (Arcadia Publishing, 2008), is possible mainly because of two people with the foresight to recognize the need for preservation of the history of our city. John Rojas, who for approximately 10 years, gathered and preserved artifacts and old photographs, and took photographs of 1980s Chula Vista. John recorded historical information from old-timers and wrote a monthly bulletin full of stories as part of his position as president of the Chula Vista Historical Society. Without John's prudence, much of the history of this area would have been lost. In 1991, the Chula Vista Library director asked Frank Roseman to start a museum in a small building in Memorial Park. He was assigned a library employee to assist him, and they gathered antique furniture and purchased display materials, slat boards, and cabinets.

The Chula Vista Library Board of Trustees funded the purchase of the materials and the painting and carpeting of the building. The museum was opened on January 1, 1992. John's photographs and artifacts were transferred from his home, garage, and yard to the Civic Center Library. The artifacts and photographs were cataloged and stored in archival boxes prior to John's unexpected death in 2000. Frank gathered additional photographs and artifacts from many sources and managed the museum he named the Heritage Museum for 10 years.

This book, like the *Chula Vista* book, would not be possible without the assistance of Donna Golden, the Chula Vista Library archivist, and Marie Aguilar of the library staff. Donna's devotion in maintaining the records of all the needed photographs allowed us to find the *then* photographs needed for this publication. Debbie Seracini, our Arcadia Publishing editor, was a source of assistance, information, and encouragement.

All the *now* photographs were generously and munificently taken by Rob E. Greenaway of Reminisce Photography. All of the aerial photographs were taken from the aircraft of Steve Buchholz that he generously provided and flew for our photographer. All the photographs in this book not otherwise noted are the property of the Chula Vista Library, Local History Collection.

INTRODUCTION

The original residents of what is now Chula Vista were Native Americans. In 1542 and 1602, the first Europeans—Spanish explorers—came to this area. The last Spanish explorer, Sebastian Vizcaino, named it San Diego Bay and sailed on. The Spanish paid little attention to San Diego until they learned that the Russians were hunting their way south along the shore of Alaska.

So 167 years after their last visit to the bay, the Spanish decided that if they wanted to claim California they needed a permanent presence there. In 1769, Fr. Junipero Serra lead a Spanish party and marched through what is now Chula Vista on the way to San Diego. Their desire was to teach the local Native Americans the Spanish culture and ways. Missions were established from San Diego to San Francisco, and the natives were taught the Christian religion, farming, building methods, and to make furniture and clothing. California had vast grazing land for the cattle the Spanish had brought with them, and soon the missions were raising thousands of head of cattle. The Native Americans did much of the work at the missions.

Under Spanish rule, the king or his representative assigned land. Most of the grazing land was assigned to the missions. Land that is now Chula Vista and the south bay was assigned to the soldiers at the Presidio for grazing their animals. The land was called El Rancho del Rey, the King's Ranch.

"New Spain" became the country of Mexico in 1821. The Mexican government gave favored men and women land grants. One such gift was to John Forster, who had married the sister of the Mexican governor of California, Pio Pico. This 26,000-acre land grant was named Rancho de la Nacion and included what is now Bonita, National City, and the western half of Chula Vista.

After the Mexican-American War, the United States took over California and allowed the land grants to continue as private property. John Forster sold the National Ranch to the Kimball brothers in 1868. Frank Kimball began developing the land as an American-style farming community. Five thousand acres south of National City were designated the agricultural farm of the Rancho; this area eventually became Chula Vista.

Kimball needed two things to have that 5,000 acres become an agricultural success. He needed transportation to the distant markets and a source of water. Kimball finally got the Sante Fe Railway to build a rail line to National City. Now having a vested interest, Sante Fe Railway financed the building of the Sweetwater Dam in 1888. Kimball now had his required sources for growing and shipping his products.

Kimball decided after experimentation that Chula Vista's crop should be lemons, as the weather near the coast was perfect for that fruit. Completion of the Sweetwater Dam allowed Chula Vista to be right in tune with the 1890s explosion of citrus production in Southern California. In 1910, Chula Vista had several thousand acres of lemon groves and declared itself the "Lemon Capital of the World."

In 1910, with a population of 550, the population of Chula Vista decided it should be a city. In 1911, the charter was adopted, and the area became the City of Chula Vista. It will soon celebrate its centennial.

Not all went well with the lemon groves; droughts, bugs, and diseases caused problems. A severe problem occurred in 1913—the Big Freeze. Most of the lemon groves were badly damaged. During the next three decades, many farmers switched to growing row crops. Celery generated the largest revenue, although tomatoes, cucumbers, lettuce, beans, and other crops were also grown.

On the eve of World War II, Chula Vista's population was 5,240 souls, and the area was primarily an agricultural community. The city's large Japanese farming population was taken away to relocation camps in the desert in April 1942, remaining there until the end of the war.

In 1940, Fred Rohr started an aircraft parts manufacturing company in San Diego. His specialty was sheet metal parts fabrication, and he had built parts for aviator Charles Lindbergh's Spirit of St. Louis. In 1941, Rohr began building a factory on the Chula Vista waterfront. The company's specialty was building metal coverings that surround aircraft engines, units called nacelles. The business started with some 800 employees and, by the height of World War II, was employing about 9,000. The B-24 bomber was manufactured in San Diego, and Rohr manufactured nacelles for thousands of these airplanes. The large working population at Rohr necessitated several wartime housing developments being built quickly. Farmland was soon covered with homes.

Thousands of service personnel passing through San Diego remembered the nice area with a fine climate, and after the war, many moved to the area and to Chula Vista. Soon homes, streets, schools, and businesses replaced lemon orchards and celery fields. In 1960, the last packinghouse was closed, and few remnants of Chula Vista's agricultural past remained. Chula Vista became a bedroom community for the San Diego area. The population grew from about 5,000 in 1940, to 44,000 in 1950, to 135,000 in 1990, and to approximately 235,000 as this was written in 2009. This is the story of Chula Vista yesteryear and today.

CHAPTER 1

VICTORIAN HOMES AND CITY VIEWS

This photograph is of a family posed on the front steps of their early orchard home in Chula Vista in the late 1800s. To the right is the orchard of lemon trees. Note the Victorian gingerbread architecture on the porch, the eave facade, and the roof. Homes of this type were abundant in the city in the late 1800s, as were the lemon groves on the properties.

Built about 1896, the Augusta Starkey house is at 21 F Street on a large property surrounded by trees the owner brought from around the world. The Starkey family owned the home from 1932 until 1990. The new owners have updated the kitchen, but the rest of the interior of the house, like the outside, remains original. The original carriage house and separate servants quarters still exist behind the main house.

This view looking east is of what was to eventually become part of Chula Vista and is the grasslands that were used by the Otay Ranch for grazing cattle. The cattle appear as dots in the lower right-hand corner of the picture above. Upper Otay Lake, which was near the Otay Ranch house, is close at left, and Lower Otay Lakes are seen farther to left in the background. The area today has been filled by the Rollin Hills development.

The James Johnson house was built in 1888 and is still at 525 F Street, a major thoroughfare. Johnson was a lemon grower, and he invented one of the first machines that could be used to wash lemons in the packinghouses. This historic Victorian home was painted in its original colors and has been faithfully maintained with its original gingerbread. That air conditioner is not the gingerbread we write of!

On the bayfront on both sides of H Street is the Rohr Aircraft Company, which was established in 1941. Below, in this southwest view over Rohr in the 1950s is one of the many mobile home parks (lower left corner) created during World War II. Rohr extends from G Street (foreground) to J Street to the left. In the upper left are the Western Salt Company ponds. The highway is the Montgomery Freeway, which was later upgraded and became Interstate 5.

This Queen Ann–style home is commonly called "The Boarding House" because that is what it was in the early lemon-growing years in Chula Vista. The need for places for the lemon grove workers to live led to the establishment of such rooms-for-rent houses. After this lovely restoration, aluminum siding and framed windows made the home more modernized, but also as it looked in the days it was built.

This above view of the Montebello Ranch centers on the Boltz home surrounded by lemon orchards, as taken in the 1920s. The driveway climbing from the lower left edge leads to the home, which still exists today. F Street rises from the lower right, and E Street/Bonita Road runs diagonally across the top. First Avenue cuts across the photograph just out of sight at the lower left. As with the rest of Chula Vista, homes have replaced the lemon groves.

This spectacular Victorian home, the Cordrey house, is at 210 Davidson Street. It originally opened to Second Avenue, but after World War II, that part of the property was subdivided, so now it opens to a side street. The architecture of the tower, set at a 45-degree angle, makes this landmark house easy to spot in aerial photographs taken many decades ago. Built in 1888, the house retains its beauty more than a century later.

This 1930s view below looks north over downtown Chula Vista along Third Avenue. The cross street at the bottom is G Street, with the Seville Theater building immediately north on Third Avenue. The First United Methodist Church of Chula Vista (built in 1912), the Community Congregational Church (enlarged in 1912), and the Carnegie Library are in the upper right-hand corner. The curved line just north of G Street indicates the turn the trains made off of Third Avenue toward Fourth Avenue. All of the aforementioned buildings are gone today.

This view over western Chula Vista is from D Street to L Street (north to south) and from First Avenue to Broadway (east to west). On the left just below center is the Chula Vista Shopping Center, and above it to the right is the Chula Vista Junior High School. H Street is across the middle of the picture. The shopping center is now much larger. The junior high school, now called a middle school, is slightly larger.

VICTORIAN HOMES AND CITY VIEWS

Above, the intersection in the foreground is that of Third Avenue (sloping downward to the right) and E Street (sloping upward to the right) in 1956. The diagonal entryway rising from the intersection leads to Fredericka Manor, a retirement home established in 1908. The modern view is looking northeast, and more units have since filled out all the open areas immediately behind Fredericka Manor. The manor was one of the first retirement homes to offer individual cottages for retired folks.

The Chula Vista Shopping Center, on Broadway between H and I Streets, was built on what was the Schertzer family farm from 1910 to 1942 and then was occupied by the Vista Square wartime housing development. Constructed in the 1960s, the larger buildings on the left were built around the Marston's store. The Sears store is on the right and is still there today, and Macy's now occupies the Marston building. Today Fifth Avenue is closed to vehicular traffic.

The historic photograph shows the original Chula Vista Community Hospital, facing F Street and bounded by Ash and Beech Streets. Two of the Watry children were born here. The Chula Vista Community Hospital has since moved to a grander set of buildings to the east of Telegraph Canyon Road, and this site is now a retirement community (pictured below). Little has changed in this neighborhood in the last four or five decades, except for the growth of the landscape.

The Tycrete Company was on G Street, which ran between its buildings, and west of Industrial Boulevard and on the bayfront. The company produced concrete blocks, kitchen counters, and other products. The hangar with "Chula Vista" written on the roof indicates this is the Chula Vista Airport, created by the Tyce brothers. Roland and Robert Tyce started the School of Aviation and provided charter service. The modern photograph shows the Rohr Aircraft Corportation/Goodrich Aerostructures, which moved onto the property in 1941.

VICTORIAN HOMES AND CITY VIEWS

The Allison Crocket house was built in 1893 and still stands at 320 Second Avenue. A Victorian-style home originally located on F Street, the house was moved so that the first Community Congregational Church could be built on the F Street site. Crocket helped to build the Congregational church that displaced his home. Some of the original gingerbread work is gone, but the basic shape and structure remain the same. The house is one of the remaining orchard homes.

The Francisco family owned this residence, located at 681 Del Mar Avenue. Their daughter, Dema, married William Peters, the owner of Peters Feed Store, and in 1914, they moved into this home. The Peters family lived there until 1971. Today, except for more landscaping, the home looks exactly the same, including the carriage house. During Chula Vista's agricultural years, the Peters Feed Store, located on Third Avenue, was very important to the farmers, growers, and cattle and horse owners.

VICTORIAN HOMES AND CITY VIEWS

This view is looking southeast over Fredericka Manor, cottages, and the McNabb Hospital. E Street is the low diagonal street, and Third Avenue is the diagonal north/south street in the photograph. Fredericka Manor was established in 1908 by Roselyn Saylor and was funded by the Timken family. All the empty lands in the historic photograph have been built out by Fredericka Manor all the way to D Street, including a large area just off to the left of the photograph.

Military housing was a necessity during World War II as many service people for the navy and marine corps came to the area and their families needed homes while they were serving elsewhere. This group of houses was built in the 1940s from east of Broadway to Fifth Avenue and from H Street to the north and I Street to the south. A much different scene appears today as various businesses and homes now fill the area.

This 1950s view of the downtown area of Chula Vista shows Fourth Avenue across the lower part of the photograph a bit beyond Park Way and Third Avenue across the top. The Chula Vista Mutual Lemon Association packing plant is on the left edge, and the trees along the wash behind the packing plant can be seen in Memorial Park. Other than the packing plants, almost all of the buildings in the historical photograph are still there a half-century later.

The Sweetwater Dam, as with most dams, is necessary where rainfall is very limited. One of the tallest dams of its kind when it was built in 1888, it has since been revised to make it even taller. The above view was taken in November 1917.

This dam supplies the water for the western half of Chula Vista, Bonita, and National City. The view of the dam face is more restrictive today due to the construction of a new toll road.

STREET SCENES

For this man, a place of rest is a large rim from a locomotive that was the city's fire alarm—used to alert volunteer firefighters of their need to attend the fire station in an emergency. From the chain hanging to the right was an iron rod used to strike (or ring) the rim. There is no need for this primitive device with all the systems of alarms used by the multiple fire stations scattered around the city.

Below, in this view looking north on Third Avenue from G Street, the Seville Service Station, Norbert Stein's Butcher of Seville Shop, and the Seville Theater are seen on the left. The first two businesses have taken the "Seville" name from the theater. A pizza parlor and the Social Security Administration offices, shaded by trees, have replaced all these buildings today. Note the arch over Third Avenue announcing Third Avenue Downtown.

On Third Avenue.. Chula Vista, California

Officers of the Chula Vista Police Department and their clerk posed with their motorcycle fleet in front of Chula Vista City Hall in this 1920s photograph. The building, constructed in 1923, housed city administration offices and the police and fire departments. That building is still there today but is now the office of the *Star-News*, the city newspaper for Chula Vista and National City. The city streets are busier, and the heavier traffic is now controlled by traffic lights.

At 317 Third Avenue is Dock's, a local gathering place since 1943. Between the *then* and *now* photographs little has changed; the sign and overhanging entryway are still that of the early years. The street has also changed little, and the same buildings still stand there, although the businesses are mostly different. Trees provide shade and make the city street more attractive, and the meters require cash to park.

Below, Fire Station No. 1, at 447 F Street, displays the "Old Goose," a 1929 pumper. The restoration of this vehicle is an ongoing task that the firefighters proudly do themselves. They use the vehicle in parades and other activities to show their pride in the old engine. Compared with today's firefighting equipment, it is a relic alongside this huge hook and ladder engine (shown above). The fire station is the same. The huge truck hides the third bay.

This business district photograph was taken at F Street looking southwest in 1936 on the west side of Third Avenue. Stores and a church are readily identifiable. Old-fashioned streetlights adorn the block. The Heller building with its decorative wrought iron balconies is similar to and across the street from the Melville building. This scene today shows the northern part of the redevelopment area of the entire block.

West Side Third Ave, Chula Vista, Calif.
Looking South

The men who labored for the Works Progress Administration (WPA) built Memorial Bowl during the Great Depression. Memorial Bowl had a large water feature and seating for several hundred people in a pleasant outdoor setting. Almost 75 years later, the water feature has been removed from Memorial Park, and a new stage enhances the facility, which is still used for city activities. Memorial Park is dedicated to fallen service personnel of four wars.

This picture from the 1920s shows the median added to the center of Third Avenue when the streetcar tracks were removed. Stores and shops along the west side of the avenue were demolished in a 1980s redevelopment project. The large buildings of Gateway Center can be seen in the distance at H Street. Now modern, beautiful buildings house shops, a restaurant, a women's fitness center, and a unisex fitness center. Modern cars date the time as 2009.

These 1950s southwest views of Chula Vista show Highway 101, which separates the farmland from the industrial area and its bridge on H Street. Highway 101 became Interstate 5 in the late 1950s. To the west, Rohr Aircraft Corporation buildings line south San Diego Bay. Almost from G Street to J Street, truck farms are evident at the base of the photograph. Today the farm area is filled with houses and businesses. Goodrich Aerostructures purchased Rohr in the 1990s.

Looking south down the center of Third Avenue from F Street in 1913 shows the trolley that ran from the Mexican border to National City via Third Avenue, Second Avenue, and E Street. The trolley and the tracks are gone, and both sides of the palm-decorated plaza are filled with stores and businesses. Note the banner on the light stanchion advertising the annual Lemon Festival, celebrating Chula Vista's reign as the "Lemon Capitol of the World."

Looking south along the east side of Third Avenue is a view taken just prior to World War II. The sign on the plaza indicates that the Fiesta de la Luna will be held on August 15, 16, and 17. The Chula Vista Women's Club started this yearly celebration in 1930. The participants were businesses that entered floats, bands from senior and junior high schools, clubs, and individuals. The same buildings are still there today.

1--The Plaza--Chula Vista, Calif.　　　　Bryan
　　　　　　　　　　　　　　　　　　　　　　Phot

Third Avenue was the main business street in Chula Vista for many years. Looking south along the east side from F Street, the Melville building is dominant on the southeast corner of the intersection. The sign at the north end of the plaza shows the mileage to nearby towns. With the Melville building still as prominent today, different shops, now shaded with trees, occupy the same buildings on the east side of the avenue.

In the 1930s, Third Avenue south of F Street had trolley tracks on the west side. The plaza has newly planted palm trees. This view shows the trolley track, which ran north from the Mexican border to National City via Third Avenue, Second Avenue, and E Street. The trolley and the tracks are gone, and Third Avenue is filled with stores and other businesses. The palms are fully grown, and the plaza remains the focal point of the avenue.

This was the Third Avenue business district in 1936. Looking southwest from F Street, the Bank of America has replaced People's Bank, a large grocery chain store has replaced the privately owned store there previously, and traffic has increased. Today the Christian Science Reading Room occupies the old Bank of America building, and a redevelopment block has replaced the older stores. Traffic lights have replaced the antique stop sign that controlled traffic in one direction.

THIRD AVE., CHULA VISTA, CAL

CHAPTER 3

CULTURE AND FAITH

This school, commonly called the Chula Vista School, was at the corner of Del Mar Avenue and F Street. Built in 1890, it was the first school constructed in Chula Vista and the only school for many years. In a north-facing view, the school is seen with a teacher and a group of students posed in front.

CARNEGIE LIBRARY
Children's room

Chula Vista's Carnegie Library was not spacious by today's standards. These libraries, especially in small towns, were magical places. Chula Vista now has three libraries, and they are more magical than ever. Computers, books on tape, microfiche readers, reading programs for all ages, and story rooms are available. This simulated trolley car, donated by the Chula Vista Friends of the Library, houses eight computer stations for children.

CULTURE AND FAITH

The F Street School, built around 1950, was a new grammar school constructed to replace the area's first school, the Chula Vista School. The F Street School is on the north side of F Street approximately one block west of the old school. This school was used until 1960. In 1976, as part of the bicentennial celebration, the Chula Vista Civic Center Library was built on the F Street school site with funds that were granted by the Johnson administration.

The Community Congregational Church was the first church and for many years the only church in Chula Vista. In 1894, the San Diego Land and Town Company deeded a church site on F Street just east of Third Avenue. Dedicated in 1894, the church was razed in 1951, and this new edifice was built at the same site. Much improved and much larger, the site is identified as Historical Site No. 5 by the City of Chula Vista.

The Otay Baptist Church is one of the oldest churches in San Diego County. It is located in Otay, a part of Chula Vista. The original building, constructed in 1890, is on the right of this photograph. It became too small and was moved and attached to a former Methodist church nearby. For 55 years, this church was without a resident pastor but was served by circuit riders.

The first Catholic church built in Chula Vista was the St. Rose of Lima Chapel, which was constructed from a structure moved from Palm City to the corner of Third Avenue and Alvarado Street in 1921. In time, the church expanded to include all the property from Alvarado Street to H Street. The church has added several planned additions, and the entire church and elementary school is now along H Street, not seen in the view below from Third Avenue.

The Carnegie Library, in this setting of parkland, is shown below just prior to its being destroyed in 1960. Its loss is still mourned by many in the city who loved the old building and would have valued it as a museum site today. Now used as a play area, much of the parkland remains south of the Norman Park Senior Center, which occupies the site. The surrounding area is fully occupied by homes.

Looking east across Fifth Avenue, Chula Vista Junior High School dominates the scene along Fifth Avenue at G Street. Built in 1927, the junior high school was surrounded by lemon groves. Pictured above in the current photograph, Vista Square Elementary School now occupies one of the lemon groves, and homes have taken over the others. The junior high school, now known as Chula Vista Middle School, still serves the community 80 years later and after many renovations.

The first school built in Chula Vista was the grammar school on F Street. Built in 1890 at the corner of Del Mar Avenue and F Street, it was the only school in Chula Vista until 1915. Above, 52 students stand in front of what was commonly known as the Chula Vista School proudly displaying the Chula Vista banner and flag. The area around the school was basically bare ground. The Norman Park Senior Center, a senior citizen facility, now occupies the site.

FIRST CHURCH CHRIST SCIENTIST
CHULA VISTA CALIFORNIA 1932

The First Church of Christ Scientist of Chula Vista, California, was built in 1928. A new church was built at 41 I Street in 1968. Christian Science churches are not dedicated until they are fully free of debt. This occurred in 1977. The Christian Science church has maintained a reading room open to the public for many years. The church is now an annex of the Southern Baptist Church, just to its west, and is used by Chinese worshipers.

The Temple Beth Sholom was originally the sanctuary of St. John's Episcopal Church. St. John's is now located farther south in a new sanctuary on First Avenue. Chula Vista's Jewish community bought this property and sanctuary, and dedicated it as Temple Beth Sholom in 1958. The temple is affiliated with the United Synagogues of Conservative Judaism. The temple serves the entire South Bay area from south of San Diego to the Mexican border.

Below, founding pastor Erling R. Jacobson admires the sign announcing his new church. Ground was broken for this new sanctuary on April 3, 1955, at Hilltop Drive and I Street. The second phase of the building occurred in 1958 and 1959 when classrooms, a youth center, and restrooms were added. In July 1962, St. Mark's Lutheran Church became part of the American Lutheran Church. In 1967, the dedication of a majestic new sanctuary and lower level classrooms was celebrated.

This is an early view of Southwestern Community College, built in 1964, looking west. Otay Lakes Road is at the lower edge of the photograph. The large building in the center is the library, and the campus was built around it. The structure in the front center is the administrative building. Today's view of the campus is extremely different with the addition of a stadium, playing fields, additional parking, and some added buildings. Home sites have increased tenfold.

This house was once a kindergarten classroom at the F Street School that stood at Fourth Avenue and F Street, the present location of the Chula Vista Civic Center Library. The first kindergarten classes were held in 1915, the same year the Chula Vista School opened. When the building was moved to 503 G Street, Alex Cameron, the owner, rented it out. The building has significance because it could be the first kindergarten classroom in the city.

Southwestern Community College held its first classes in 1961 in the evenings at the Chula Vista High School on Fifth Avenue and did so for several years. Southwestern Community College, at the corner of Otay Lakes Road and H Street, is a two-year community education facility that opened its campus and held its first classes there on September 11, 1964. As with most new facilities, the grounds, built on farmland, were bare of vegetation. Today the campus is a beautiful, grassy, tree-covered, student-filled college.

The F Street School, an elementary school, was occupied from 1916 to 1960. F Street is across the lower part of the photograph below, next to the ball field at lower right, and Fourth Avenue is on the left. The F Street School was the only elementary school in Chula Vista from 1916 until 1938. On this site is the new Chula Vista Civic Center Library (built in 1976) and the Will T. Hyde Friendship Park.

CULTURE AND FAITH

CHAPTER 4

STRICTLY
COMMERCIAL

In the early 1900s, Chula Vista was at the zenith of its self-described title as "Lemon Capitol of the World." Lemon orchards were in abundance. Several lemon-packing plants were kept busy packing and shipping lemons by rail all over the country. The women on this packing line are sorting and packing the fruit in divided boxes.

Just west of Third Avenue at the corner of Landis Street was Arnold's Garage, a familiar sight for several decades. Arnold's served the community in the care of their cars, trucks, and trailers. The business was welcomed, appreciated, and necessary. The garage was there from 1946 until 1980 when redevelopment took the property. Marie Callendar's, a popular restaurant, now fills the site that was part of the redevelopment of the whole block area.

STRICTLY COMMERCIAL

Below, workers on this B-24 radial engine line at Rohr Aircraft Corporation are mounting exterior aerodynamic structure and attendant equipment to an engine supplied by another manufacturer. The finished product is a ready-to-mount power package called a nacelle. These products were taken by truck to Consolidate Vultee Aircraft on Harbor Drive in San Diego for mounting. Goodrich Aerostructures, now occupying the Rohr site, does the same operations on engines supplied by another, but on a vastly different type of aircraft engine.

Below, this garage was a fixture on F Street for six decades. Rex Fuson began working for Herb Bryant in 1921. The garage specialized in repairing auto electrical systems and radios. More interested in radios, Bryant sold the business to Fuson in 1922. From then until closing, the garage was operated by three generations of Fusons. A large, modern office building with businesses on the ground floor and resident apartments above has replaced what once was a landmark.

The People's State Bank, once housed in the Melville building, moved to this location diagonally across Third Avenue to this new building. This bank later became the Bank of America. The Christian Science Reading Room now occupies the bank building, and the avenue is more shopper-friendly with shade trees and benches. Informational plaques, like the one seen in the foreground, are scattered around the entire area. The local newspaper office is in the third building to the right.

The Security Trust and Savings Bank moved into the Melville building after the People's State Bank moved across the street. The Security Bank moved to the corner of Church Street and F Street, and the attractive and much-consulted clock moved as well. The clock today enhances the First Pacific Trust Bank on that corner. The Melville building has different businesses in it—a dental office has replaced the bank, and a collectors and frame shop has replaced the bakery.

STRICTLY COMMERCIAL

The Hercules Powder Company, an eastern manufacturer of explosives and munitions, built this expansive plant in1916 at the bayfront to process kelp from the La Jolla giant kelp beds. The kelp processors have been replaced in what is now the Sweetwater National Wildlife Refuge by the Chula Vista Nature Center. The center opened in 1978 and is nationally recognized as a zoo and aquarium that exhibits plants, animals, and fish that are native to the San Diego area.

The Chula Vista Citrus Association, a member of the Sunkist Growers, owned the largest lemon-packing plant in Chula Vista. It was located at the southeast corner of Third Avenue and K Street. It was in business from 1918 until 1960 and shipped Chula Vista lemons all over the country by refrigerated railcars. A Bank of America branch has replaced the packing plant, and the area has long been occupied by homes and businesses.

C.V. CITRUS ASSOCIATION PLANT – ca. 1940
Corner of Third Avenue and K Street
Packing House for "Sunkist" Lemons

Robert "Bob" Tyce at the Chula Vista Airport is pictured above, standing next to his Hispano-Suisse Jenny. Bob and his brother Roland "Rolly" were both pilots and used the airstrip along the San Diego bay south of G Street at the convenience of the railroad. Bob moved to Honolulu and opened a flying service. He was killed during the Japanese attack on Pearl Harbor. Below, Steve Buchholz, a flying instructor flew a photographer in his Aeronca Chief to take the *now* photographs in this book.

Farrell's general store and the United States
Post Office were located at the corner of Center
Street and Third Avenue in 1911. The unpaved
streets in the center of the town and use of the
horses and wagons attest to the early beginnings
of Chula Vista. The only horses in town now are
under the hood of the automobiles. In 1980, the
redevelopment block replaced the general store
and the other old buildings.

STRICTLY COMMERCIAL

Below, this business district—one of several on Broadway in the 1950s—was on the east side of the street and south of E Street. A paint store (far left), a store being readied for opening, a restaurant advertising lunch, an appliance store, and a furniture store offer the complete shopping choices. Little has changed on this block. The storefronts are much the same except for the Chinese restaurant facade on the old restaurant and the different businesses.

Zontek's Fine Foods, a café around 1940, was a popular eating place at 213 Third Avenue and was next to another popular place, a card room called Chub's Club. It appears much has changed in this area of the block, but it is mainly different facades on the same buildings. The public street art on the right is one of several along the avenue. Chub's and Zontek's have been replaced by a jewelry store, a shoe store, and a bakery.

In the early 1900s, the Pure Gold packinghouse was at the corner of Center Street and Fourth Avenue. The F Street School is seen at the top left of the above picture, and the baseball playing field is between the school and the packinghouse. Directly to the right rear of the packinghouse is the railroad that allowed the convenient shipping of lemons to market. Presently, an apartment complex named Parkwoods occupies the site along Fourth Avenue.

The Western Salt Works, in business since 1870, is located on the south end of San Diego Bay. Its salt, which was taken from ponds separated by levees, is seen in the storage piles. Little has changed, and the shaker building that breaks up the salt crystals is still operating as it has for many years. The harvesting of salt is slightly different, and the shipping is now by truck rather than railcars. Salt for home use is no longer made.

The Melville building is often mentioned in Chula Vista publications because of it significance to Third Avenue. Built in 1911 at the corner of Third Avenue and F Street, it appears the same today except for its missing window facades. Instead of streetcar tracks, a center island decorated with palm trees occupies the middle of the avenue. The picture below was taken before the flood of 1916 that washed out the tracks over the Sweetwater River. Different businesses now occupy the building.

It may be remembered that in 1922 Herb Bryant sold his automobile garage on F Street to Rex Fuson because he was more interested in things electric. Bryant set up his electrical business on the northeast corner of F Street and Third Avenue to service and sell radios, and to also sell electrical supplies. Those buildings are still there today. The large tree hides the tall building that was the furniture store. Bryant's old store is the newly decorated one at the corner.

This Bank of America building is at 444 Third Avenue, and the operation was previously located at both 300 and 255 Third Avenue. The picture above was taken at the corner of Third Avenue and E Street during a 1950s holiday season. The building today has a new logo and a new brick facade, and its location is still on one of the busiest corners in the city. The Bank of America has a second bank building farther south on Third Avenue.

This was Chula Vista in 1960. This view looking north from about Center Street toward F Street shows the many shops and businesses on each side of the avenue. The ever-present plaza and its palm trees that have grown to a greater height decorate the scene. Congregational Tower, a modern senior residence, is the tallest building in the city and stands on F Street. The many businesses along Third Avenue are in the same buildings with little change to their appearance.

CHAPTER 5

PUBLIC FACILITIES

Chula Vista's first library was a collection of books donated by its citizens. Andrew Carnegie, a major steel-industry tycoon in the late 1800s and a philanthropist to small cities in America in the early 1920s where it concerned education, granted funds for the building of libraries. Chula Vista was one of the cities that received such a grant.

The U.S. Post Office in Chula Vista was located at 315 Third Avenue on December 1942. Being located in the shopping district made it convenient for the people to access the post office. Upgraded from delivery by horse and buggy, these Christmas packages will be delivered by open automobile sedans loaded (one might say) to the ultimate. These buildings are all much the same but with different occupants and updated facades.

The McCoy Hotel was located close to the southeast corner of Landis Avenue and F Street. Its grounds were bare with what looks like grading equipment parked on the front "lawn." Buildings to the rear and to the barn to the left are part of the property. Again the redevelopment of the 30 block from F Street south has replaced the hotel with offices, a school, and a Women's Fitness World.

The Seville Theater was the first and only entertainment venue in Chula Vista for many years. Its location near the business center of Third Avenue made it readily accessible to children for Saturday matinees and to families for evening movies. Neighboring businesses took the Seville name and used it as their own: for example, the Butcher of Seville for a butcher shop. The Social Security Administration offices, which take up almost the complete block, have replaced the theater and the other buildings.

Chula Vista's Carnegie Library, like others of the 1,679 Carnegie libraries built between 1886 and 1921, was a great addition to a small town. A magical place today for the area's senior citizens is the Norman Park Senior Center, which stands in the space the Carnegie Library occupied. With spacious rooms for meetings, games, dances, and exercise equipment, the senior center also has a reading area, a poolroom, and shuffleboard courts available to all who join.

In the 1950s, the U.S. Post Office was located in a group of public government buildings at 299 Guava Avenue. The entrance to the building was on Guava Avenue, and F Street was on the south side of the building. To the north of the post office was the city library, built in 1956. The post office building has been replaced on Fourth Avenue by a new administration building in the renovated City Center Complex.

El Primero Hotel, built in 1930 and owned by John and Lily Radcliffe, is an example of Zag Moderne architecture. The next owners left the hotel to fall into disrepair during the years of their ownership. In an attempt at restoration, the exterior was painted in bizarre, dramatic, unpleasing colors. The new owners have restored and updated the interior and have returned the exterior to the original colors.

The first Chula Vista hospital was at 590 Third Avenue at the corner of I Street. It was a facility that could accommodate four patients and had nurse attendants on three shifts. Any licensed physician could place his patients there for care. San Diego County built a new assessor's office in that space in 1995 and did business there for about six years, or until 1991. A realty office occupies the space today.

Built around 1911, the Chula Vista City Hall on Third Avenue also served as the fire and police stations. Below, the firefighters proudly display the city fire department equipment. The small truck to the right was the city's first piece of fire apparatus. It was a fire truck with a hose and a pumper, and it served as the fire chief's vehicle. The buildings identifiable today are, to the far left, the old bank building, and the second-story windows identify another building. The *Star-News*, the city newspaper, occupies part of the building that was once city hall.

Below, the Chula Vista City Hall built in 1951 was on Guava Avenue and was part of the Chula Vista Civic Center Complex. It had the offices of the city council, the council chambers, and offices for staff. The tower to the left was the communications antenna for the fire department.

After a complete interior renovation, the city hall looks much the same but is surrounded by all new buildings. These buildings house everything but the police department, which is on F Street along Fourth Avenue.

The 1956 Chula Vista Library was in the Chula Vista Civic Center, north of the U.S. Post Office, facing Davidson Street. It was built to take the place of the Carnegie Library on F Street. It served the city until the new Chula Vista Civic Center Library was built on F Street in 1976. The new library used federal revenue-sharing funds supplied to cities from the Johnson administration to construct the building. Chula Vista chose to use the entire grant for one building.

The Vogue Theater, at 230 Third Avenue, was the second theater in Chula Vista. Tom Huntingdon had this theater built in 1945 and owned and operated it. The theater was active for many years as the only theater after the Seville Theater, located farther south on Third Avenue, closed. The Vogue Theater recently closed and was sold. It was renovated but is not currently operating.

PUBLIC FACILITIES

The San Diego and Arizona Eastern Railroad Station was located in the heart of the Chula Vista business district at Third Avenue and Park Way. In the picture below, the station, although closed, was maintained as a reminder of what was for people not here when the railroad tracks were on Third Avenue. Today the corner vacated by the railroad station is at the edge of Memorial Park, a place dedicated to local veterans who have fallen in battle.

The San Diego County Judicial Building housed the South Branch of the San Diego County Municipal Court. The building was part of the Chula Vista Civic Center Complex at 260 Fourth Avenue. The building was used by the city for other purposes after the court closed. When the Chula Vista Civic Center was renovated a few years ago, the building was torn down. The new building is occupied by the Chula Vista Finance Department.

PUBLIC FACILITIES

This is the facade of the Chula Vista Junior High School at 415 Fifth Avenue on the corner of G Street. Part of the facility was damaged by fire some time ago and was restored and renovated. The school has a large playing field in the rear for its gym classes. Now called a middle school with 1,128 students for grades seven and eight, it is one of 17 middle schools in the Sweetwater Union School District.

These students from Chula Vista High School are participating in their graduation ceremony on June 15, 1949, in Memorial Bowl, a section of Memorial Park. The students in their caps and gowns are standing in front of the decorated dressing-room building that was on the stage when plays were presented there. The water feature and the building are gone today. The stage was replaced, and the decorative structure was added, but the amphitheater and seating remained the same.

This aerial view of Southwestern Community College, looking west, has the library as the central building surrounded by the remainder of the campus. This picture was taken when the two-year college was relatively new and had little landscaping. Today the grounds are well decorated with trees, shrubs, and grass areas for student lounging. Additional parking has been added to accommodate the increase in student enrollment. Many homes have been built nearby, and there are businesses to serve them.

www.arcadiapublishing.com

Discover books about the town where you grew up, the cities where your friends and families live, the town where your parents met, or even that retirement spot you've been dreaming about. Our Web site provides history lovers with exclusive deals, advanced notification about new titles, e-mail alerts of author events, and much more.

Find Your Place in History.